### Read-About® Math

# Slumber Party Problem Solving

## By Brian Sargent

**Consultants**
Chalice Bennett
Elementary Specialist
Martin Luther King Jr. Laboratory School
Evanston, Illinois

Ari Ginsburg
Math Curriculum Specialist

Children's Press®
A Division of Scholastic Inc.
New York   Toronto   London   Auckland   Sydney
Mexico City   New Delhi   Hong Kong
Danbury, Connecticut

Designer: Herman Adler Design
Photo Researcher: Caroline Anderson
The photo on the cover shows a girl making a list of problems to solve
before her slumber party starts.

**Library of Congress Cataloging-in-Publication Data**

Sargent, Brian, 1969–
　Slumber party problem solving / by Brian Sargent.
　　p. cm. — (Rookie read-about math)
　ISBN 0-516-24962-2 (lib. bdg.)　0-516-29829-1 (pbk.)
　1. Arithmetic—Juvenile literature. 2. Problem solving—Juvenile
literature. I. Title. II. Series.
　QA115.S273 2006
　513—dc22
　　　　　　　　　　　　　　　　　　2005019650

CHILDREN'S PRESS, and ROOKIE READ-ABOUT®,
and associated logos are trademarks and/or registered trademarks
of Scholastic Library Publishing. SCHOLASTIC and associated logos
are trademarks and/or registered trademarks of Scholastic Inc.

1 2 3 4 5 6 7 8 9 10 R 15 14 13 12 11 10 09 08 07 06

I'm having a slumber
party tonight!

Slumber parties are fun.

I have some problems
I need to solve before
the party starts.

I've made a list of them.

# Problem #1: Time

I'm a little worried.

# Do I have enough time to clean up for the party?

It is 4:00 p.m. now. The party starts at 6:00 p.m.

How many hours do I have to get ready?

Six minus four is two. I have two hours. Great! That's plenty of time!

$6 - 4 = 2$

9

# Problem #2: Sleeping Bags

How many sleeping bags do we need? How many do we have?

We keep the sleeping bags in a closet. Let's go look.

We have four sleeping bags.

I invited three friends.
Three friends plus me
equals four people.

3 + 1 = 4

There is one sleeping
bag for each person.
No problem there!

## Problem #3:
## Stuffed Animals

I want each of us to have one stuffed animal for the night.

I have seven stuffed animals.

How many stuffed animals should I put back on my bed?

I have seven
stuffed animals.

Four people need
stuffed animals.

Seven minus four
equals three.

Three stuffed animals
go back on my bed.

$7 - 4 = 3$

I've solved three problems. There is one more problem on the list.

## Problem #4: Food

How much pizza do we need? That's a tough one.

I usually eat about two slices. Each friend eats two slices, too.

Four groups of two slices each equals eight slices in all.

$4 \times 2 = 8$

One pizza has eight slices. That means we need one pizza.

Uh-oh, there is one problem I forgot to put on the list.

How many pillows do we need for the pillow fight?

# Words You Know

list

pillows

pizza

problem

sleeping bags

slumber party

stuffed animals

time

31

# Index

# About the Author

Brian Sargent is a middle-school math teacher. He lives in Glen Ridge, New Jersey, with his wife Sharon and daughters Kathryn, Lila, and Victoria. He usually eats four slices of pizza.

# Photo Credits